SANCTIFIED SUFFERING:

A NEW WAY TO WALK VICTORIOUSLY IN CHRIST!

I0559756

Author Lynette Costner

ISBN: 978-1-963502-24-4

"This book is a MUST HAVE! It is wise, powerful and provides a new deep perspective when you are grieving and feel desperate for some hope!!! It is a life-changer!"

Dr. Kimberly Ventus-Darks, International Motivational Speaker, Author & Purpose Guru

Special Thanks...

To my mom, Pastor Cordelia Nowell:
You showed me how to triumph against all odds. Your faithfulness to your relationship with God was very strong. He answered many of your prayers because of it. Rest in Paradise

To my godmother, Marilyn Foulkes:
God gave you a gift of selflessness and love for others. Grateful for you loving me through my darkest sufferings. Rest in Paradise

To my daughters, Kristen Price and Dr Lauren Price. Both of you were my rock in both the good and bad times. God has been faithful to us through our sufferings and continues to elevate us more.

The meaning of suffering is for you to die and then be reborn again!

Table of Contents

ARE WE ADDICTED TO SUFFERING?

CHP 1

Is part of the current dream of the planet…

Terrorist attacks, mass shootings, wars, etc

Are all examples of this,

And until we as a species recognize the addiction to suffering, these situations will continue to resurface. That being said, it is still possible for us to see the beauty that coexists in the world, even at the same time that great suffering is present.

— DON JOSE RUTZ

In God's flawless perspective, there is nothing *too big or too small,* the knowledge of size as we know it, doesn't exist. If we are concerned about it, then God is concerned about it!

There is no compromise to this truth.

AMEN & AMEN!

This truth extends to all segments in our walk with Christ. Our Christian faith will go as high as we allow it to go. It has no limits unless we put limits to it. God does not restrain it; we are the ones with the boundaries. We tend to get into the habit of doing what other people do. And we are comfortable when we think how other people think. Even in our Christian circles we allow others to influence how high we will go in God. When we look at our Christian mentors, we often hope to one day have their perspective, faith and walk with Christ. We allow the height of their walk to influence how far we should go. We allow them to be our ultimate model instead of allowing Christ to be our superior standard. Unfortunately, if we tend to be get too radical in our faith, we allow the seasoned Christians to influence our thinking and behavior to a more normal and realistic level of faith. We yearn to fit and feel comfortable in our spiritual circles. Allowing others to dictate how to be normal in God, is why we have so many Christians unaware of their potential gifts and available power they could possess.

"To think health when surrounded by the appearances of disease,

Or to think riches when in the midst of appearances of poverty, requires power,

But whoever acquires this power becomes a MASTERMIND."

Wallace D. Wattles

<u>BEWARE: Comfort Is the Beginning of Addiction!</u>

The word comfortable is very dangerous and deceptive in the Spiritual Realm. In this world of chaos, violence, pandemics, and poverty we are desperate to be understood and included. We tell ourselves that we really don't care what people think. But we care, very strongly we care. Everything about our faith walk is designed to stretch us to a higher level which automatically brings a lack of comfort and unfamiliarity. This simple and overlooked word has become an invisible stronghold to what we expect, what we ask for, and ultimately what we get from God. *Let me be clear, peace is not being comfortable. Peace is when you can hold on to your sense of calm in the midst of great suffering and discomfort!*

Despite the promises God has guaranteed, we would be astonished if we realized how we have so easily settled for what we expect from God. We have allowed our habits and everyday normalcy blindly pull us into this mediocre expectation that the world lives by. Living in the world physically while staying focused on God spiritually, is almost impossible without having a radical commitment to Christ. This balance we unconsciously try to achieve is often due to the need to be comfortable. Even as sold-out Christians, we have a constant need to be understood. God, in all of His wisdom, put this desire in us, so that we can bond, love and have meaningful relationships. Without this need to connect, we would be like robots, not connecting or caring about anyone or anything.

This craving to be comfortable is a word that the enemy uses to distract us and tempt us throughout our entire life journey. As Christians, we often don't discuss this misguided need. But much of the hardships that we allow ourselves to get entangled in, comes from outside

peer pressure and inside emotional pressure to bond.
The need is much more powerful than we realize.
Many experts believe that acceptance by peers is the number one thing that teenagers desire.

Living physically on earth while mentally getting everything you need from God, is something we can't accomplish without the power of God. We can't balance Christ with Earth. It is impossible to balance your spiritual journey on a balance beam. *Listen closely, Christ can't be measured or compared to anything or anyone. Nothing and absolutely no-one can share the same space with our Eternal Father. We are guilty of trying to bring God down to our need, understanding and comfort level instead of growing higher to His.*

 Unfortunately, we live in a state of desiring constant comfort. Even in our daily walk, we are used to having the option of changing our decisions in our life until we are at peace.

How we think, is not how God thinks. Too many of us believe that we are more God-focused than what we really are. We have come to believe that if God is in our decisions partially, that we have given Him control entirely, and this is simply not true. We need to recognize that the main reason Christians are not more radical in their faith is the uncomfortableness it brings. We live in a world where the majority of people are either anti-God or crisis-based believers. Society will still accept you if you attend church and occasionally pray for others who are in trouble. As long as, you don't try to save souls or become "Crazy in Jesus" you are not a threat and others see you as being a reasonable believer. So, when you have one foot on Earth and the other in Heaven, the constant influence, and the seductive nature of sin; compared to the loving, peaceful personality of holiness, usually wins. Due to the fact, we can physically see what the world has to offer the sinful nature of others seem so fun and freeing, it is a fight every day not to be pulled in by the greed of the world. If you don't stay guarded, you will find that even though you are saved, the results of your life will resemble more world influence than spirit conviction. When this happens your faith and vision of what God can do in your life in times of trouble, becomes more and more blurry! In your suffering, you start seeing and confessing things that society would say and do. And before you know it, common and faithless words become part of your vocabulary. For example, "It probably won't work out, Things look hopeless as usual, or I hate my life!" Unless you are coated around other believers who believe and confess that God will keep them and restore them regardless of what is in their future, your vision of God can easily drift farther and farther away.

What I am saying is the desperate need to be included and the overwhelming desire to have a sense of normalcy and comfort around us is a major reason we slip in our faith. Think about it, if everyone was a Christian there would not be a challenge being one too. But because you are going against the grain, of what others think is acceptable, we battle with what side of us we

Want to show to the world!

If you listen to the tone of past comments and the negativity that so easily spools out of the mouth of others, it is usually filled with a hopeless and powerless tone.

In fact, when we hear someone that is super positive, energetic, and talks constantly optimistic, many of us are caught off guard. In fact, as a society we tend to not like someone that only shows excitement and positivity. We often don't trust them. And we are quick to call them fake. We prejudged them as being silly, unrealistic, or simply dreamers.

The world celebrates those who are addicted to suffering. Our society is much more favorable to people who will deal with the suffering directly. It is hard to tolcratc thosc who try to overcome suffering by lying to themselves that grief does not exist.

It is time that we become more transparent because with one foot in the world and one foot searching for heaven, we are caught in a two-faced truth where we don't totally trust God, but we know we need more than what the world offers.

Society also tends to use suffering as an excuse not to do better and not to try harder. Please don't misunderstand me, we don't want to suffer. But we have become accustomed to being happy for a moment and then our once happy life turns bad resulting in a deep continual stream of disappointment. Christians and non-Christians often find it hard to put their guard down and enjoy the happiness they are experiencing. Somewhere deep in our heart we are fearful of trusting that our life will stay happy. Life has become so unpredictable, and the world changes are so constant and scary that many of us live constantly guarded, waiting for our troubles to consume us again.

We are addicted to suffering.

Many people find it easier to start preparing for the suffering process before the grief even comes. So many of us find it more comforting to not allow ourselves to totally grasp on the good. But instead, not to allow ourselves to trust and enjoy the full happiness of our pleasure. We do this as a guard, so the disappointment won't be so horrific when the problems come!

The Christian's Blueprint

It is important to realize as Christians that God gave us the need to bond so that we can live, love, and have strong relationships. Our Father's ultimate plan was for us to have the very thing we now battle for. His desire was for us to live a life that is predictable, consistently joyful and without grieving. He never wanted us to live a life so cautiously, that even in our joyful times we are overwhelmed with the fear that trouble was lurking by, to destroy our pleasure. But due to the great fall of Adam and Eve, we must always remember that the enemy is out to exaggerate every bad experience in our life. He is especially concerned about serious believers. He tries very hard to strategically make us see the outcome of our life just like those that are not believers. His desire is for our feet to be more in the world then in heaven. The enemy wants to demolish us through destroying our faith and obliterating our testimony. It is his goal to make us more and more dependent on being comfortable so that we will lose our interest in the things of God; therefore, becoming more and more addicted to the habits of the world.

****

If we are not guarded the enemy will use the advantages that Christ gives us, like comfort and peace and place a fake substitute out in the world, to lessen our dependence on God.

****

Finally, it is natural to get comfortable with living here on earth. But let us remember that we are here to fulfill a purpose. Each of us has an assignment to do. So, we need to lessen our need to be accepted by people, because our true mission is to not to seek comfort from others, but to give comfort to others.

WHAT YOU NEVER KNEW ABOUT SUFFERING

CHP 2

Suffering has no eyes so it can not see you

Suffering has no heart so it can not feel you

It does not come to devastate you because of your color, gender, or social status.

It has no prejudice. It does not like anyone, it does not care.

It is universal, it affects everyone. You can't escape it, where you hide, it will get there first. It will always exist because it has no life span. The ultimate fall at the beginning allowed it to enter in, so as long as the world exist, it will exist too. Although you can't control when it comes, you can be guarded before it comes. The intensity of it depends on your spiritual weapons you have stored.

As Christians one of the hardest life adjustments, we must make is living in this world physically while still being focused on Spiritual promises mentally. We make a common mistake of being "all in" in some of the more basic areas of faith, while completely missing God in the more complex situations that aren't discussed, in our Christian circles.

I believe that we would be more successful in times of suffering if we realized that suffering is one of the most powerful and all-consuming strongholds that we endure. It pushes us to our lowest point of existence. Many times, it is the grief in the suffering where we start hoping, wishing, and praying that our life will end. It truly is the place where we witness who we really are when we are stripped, broken and have nothing left. *It is one of the most common times that we either run toward God or quickly escape from Him.* Oftentimes, everything we have built up to believe and do stops instantly in the presence of suffering. It is automatic. Our life and all that we thought we knew just stops, instantly.

Suffering Latches on You!

Through my own personal experience, I will be the first to say that suffering is something that you quite never get over. We have learned to put band aids over our wounds, but the pain of the sore stays with us. We think that we have overcome the hurt but when hurt in other areas come, the staining of suffering starts to seep through again. It feels like we are on the edge of reverting back to that same feeling of grief for the rest of our life. It becomes our target area. The reason for our sadness and often the basis for lifetime depression.

So, when pain from our everyday life happens, the source of our suffering tends to come out of its hiding place too.

Pain Attracts Pain!

So, when the pain of being talked about or misunderstood comes, the feelings of hurt, anger and rejection are doubled. As Christians, we would see our suffering differently and with more balance, if we understood that the source of our suffering may always affect us, because it tends to latch on to our present hurt too.

Have you ever shocked yourself when you took gossip or lies that someone said about you really hard? You knew you were being super sensitive, but you just could not shake the feeling of your hurt?

So often we are stunned at how hard we suffer from small things. We become frustrated because we feel that we should be stronger and better. But as Christians we need to realize that emotional pain on any level often doubles in hurt. We don't realize that the past suffering will often come alive and alert in the presence of any level of present pain if we have not been fully healed from past suffering.

When I reflect on the suffering of my own life, I have often asked questions about how to sustain my grief. Although this period of agony was the worst time in my life, God looked way beyond how I felt. Through His grace, He keeps us and is constantly reminding us of the power of his love during our darkest time. But because

God is God. He takes my emotion out of my suffering and instead He sees it as a time of breaking, total transparency, and a clear path to seek Him completely.

Regardless of if it feels like it or not, suffering is spiritual! When you take out of the human side of it, it really comes down to you and God! Often times, suffering is the only way to get closer to our Father. It is through our grief that causes us to break from ourselves and become empty before God!

As a Christian when grief happens, many of us start transferring over to the worldly perspective of anger, blame and hopelessness. But regardless of how it may feel at the time, Gods desire is for us to become stronger, better, and bolder so we can be more prepared for our future assignments that He has planned for us.

Romans 8:17 says "Now if we are children, then we are heirs with Christ, if indeed we share in his sufferings in order that we may also share in his glory."

3 WAYS TO SANCTIFY YOUR SUFFERING

CHP 3

Don't Resist: Respect & Bow to Your New Reality

Suffering is one of the few things that commands instant priority. It creates an instant STOP to everything you thought you had planned. Now there are many ways we can explain this phrase, but I am using it as a way to pause, pay attention to, or to become immediately aware of your present circumstance.

"Time Stops When Suffering Comes"

Let's be clear, if you are a Christian or not, universally we often battle with the same challenges, situations, and fears. Think about it, most of us are overworked, exhausted, and want more. In order to pay our bills and maintain our current status we live every day in a habitual sort of lifestyle.

We see without really seeing

We live without really living

We become creatures of habits

Until a tragedy shocks us back to reality!

The pattern of getting up, going to work, coming home, and then going back to bed, just to go to work again is more realistic than most of us want to admit. Most of us have driven to work on autopilot not remembering what

route we took to get there. It's not unusual for us to plop medication in our mouth and 15 minutes later, trying to recall if we really took it or not. Life has bombarded us with so much "this and that" that our brain often escapes to a "blurry lockdown phase" just for us to remain sane and able to function!!!

The impact and shock of an unfortunate and unexpected tragedy has enough power that it will wake us up instantly from our fog. *We physically might be present but where we are mentally is truly where we are.* For example, our blood pressure is not affected by where our steps lead us. But our blood pressure lives parallel to the intensity of our thoughts and the peace that we don't have. *If we are not present mentally, we are not truly there.*

Sometimes, God allows a tragedy to happen because that is the only way we would stop, pause, and be redirected.

Finally, true happiness requires some suffering. For example, a drug addict receives temporary happiness from chemical drugs which results in limited satisfaction. This temporary happiness over time creates devastating problems which impacts families, money, losses and possibly imprisonment. The crisis becomes the uncontrollably need for this temporary pleasure at all costs.

The Christian's Blueprint

Since our past pain clusters with future pain, sometimes it can be almost impossible to know where our pain is coming from. The enemy likes to confuse us and keep us in a life of blind suffering. So that we blame God for our confusion and hopelessness. He does not want us to know that "Pain activates Pain." As Christians we need to pray that God will reveal the source of what we are really dealing with.

We must stop assuming we know, when in actuality the experience of suffering is deeper than what we can ever truly understand.

We need to give up trying to completely understand the why or the how our suffering came, it is something that we are not equipped to truly understand. We should sanctify our pain by knowing that God will make a blessing out of the things that hurt us the most!

James 1:12 ESV "Blessed is the man who remains steadfast under trial, for when he has stood the test he will receive the crown of life, which God has promised to those who love him.

1 Peter 5:10 ESV And after you have suffered a little while, the God of all grace, who has called you to his eternal glory in Christ, will himself restore, confirm, strengthen, and establish you.

****

Do not despise suffering. It reminds you that you are on a pilgrimage to a far better place. It does provide some pleasures and comforts along the way, but they are temporary. When you reach your final destination-your home in heaven-I will shower you with pleasures forevermore. In that glorious place there will be no more death or mourning or crying or pain. The fullness of joy you experience there will be permanent, never-ending.

Because you are My treasured follower, I can promise that your suffering will come to an end someday. Therefore, try to view your trouble as momentary and light -producing for you as an eternal weight of Glory beyond all measure and surpassing all comparison!

While you continue your journey through this world, be thankful for the comforts and pleasures I bless you with. Reach out to others who are suffering. I comfort you in all your troubles so that you can comfort others. Offering help to hurting people gives meaning to your suffering—and Glory to Me!

Allow Your Sanctification to Snatch Away All Fears

True suffering can bring out emotional truths in us we never knew we had. Depending on the level of suffering it can do much for the building up and the breaking down of our character. When we are instantly forced to go into a state of deep suffering, we are using everything in us just to survive and to physically make it from hour to hour. We are unaware of the other part of our body that is searching for normalcy, calm and peace. When we are in an unusual emotional state other parts of our body reacts in another entirely different direction to keep us going. Our emotional state might be losing grip and trying to keep us sane, but our spiritual mind is trying hard to help us to remember to lean on the strength of God. Our Father has equipped us with a remarkable body that can be in pain and heal itself at the same time.

We think we know who we are and how we will react at our lowest point, but we simply don't know. We underestimate the amazing and indescribable body that

God has given to us. Unless we have experienced it, most of us really don't know how we would react in our darkest moment. We can speculate and envision it, but most of us don't really know.

Depending on what it is, suffering can make you feel like you are ready to quit life, take your last breath and never ever turn back. But it can also cause a strange incredible sense of GODLY PROTECTION. A place where 100% of the Father is walking with you with every single step. The place where every fear you have ever had has to go. A place where all anxiety just vanishes away.

God's glory is everywhere, so even the fears you had at another time and for a different reason must submit to Him. Everything ceases when it comes to the glory of our King. Nothing else makes sense except our Father! All your doubts, fears and anxiety has just disappeared. The closer you are to God the calmer and freer you feel. The brokenness we experience is more God than pain, and more God than anything else allows you to extend to the highest place in your relationship with God.

On the other hand, grief is double sided. It can knock you down so low that you aren't concerned about the outcome anymore. That your only real desire is to just stay kept and protected. That nothing more than staying anchored in God is what consumes your thoughts.

What I am saying is, suffering can get to the point that you are no longer looking at the problem. But your focus is solely on Christ. It will give you the confidence that covers all your past fears and doubts. You will be fully convinced that there is absolutely nothing or anyone that you should fear any longer.

The Glory of God shows you that all things are made by Him, and all things are His. As Christians, when we are protected by the most High in everything we do, we have nothing to fear or be concerned about. For us to get to this place, it oftentimes takes the most brutal circumstance for us to see All God and No Self. Everyday challenges can't get us to that height. Only when we go through the most brutal and shocking situations of suffering will the ultimate NO FEAR OF ANYTHING introduce itself.

This too Shall Pass & Trouble don't last Always, are words of encouragement that we use to strengthen one another in times of great grief and personal challenge! Although we know this is true and that someday we will feel some relief, let's be real, when you are the one counting the days and waiting until the storm passes through, there are few words that can bring comfort to any part of the suffering. Although we know that "trouble don't last always" most of us want some type of promise that our life will get back to a sense of normalcy again. That there will be more joy, in our life than pain.

Most of us have been in strange and precarious situations that has shocked us into an unfamiliar emotional state of desperation. We can become so fed up with the suffering that we really don't care what happens with the outcome. It is a time when we truly let go of the situation and let God. We stop crying, trying and constructing how we want things to work out. We just stop trying to guide God's hand, we lose our motivation and tell ourselves that this must be fixed by God! This often happens when we have hoped, prayed,

29

and believed for relief and answers so much that our believing has become more of a habit, than a statement of belief and confession.

While living in this world already filled with an overwhelming since of violence, sickness, and unfairness; along with our own personal grief regarding the world's constant growing problems, can make living seems almost unbearable. *A deep feeling of grief and suffering that leaves you feeling that you have nothing else to live for can drain your emotions so bad that your feelings of fear and anxiety just disappear into a feeling of: "I don't care anyway."*

Our constant state of grief starts becoming our normal and we start living with the life that we have been left with. After some time, it becomes our new normal.

Many people have a hard time believing that Christ really does want the best for us. He wants us to be as joyous and peaceful as we possibly can as we live here in this world. The feeling of giving up and letting go of what your life was and what you wanted it to be. Living out a life where you are not denying the suffering or hiding from the pain. You are no longer bothered or troubled, is where Christ wants us to be.

But regardless of our relationship with God, most of us have mastered the *holding on more than the letting go.* Although the pain is unbearable, we have learnt to still try to handle the outcome, regardless of what we talk and preach about saying all our strength comes from the most High.

The Suffering can be the Best of Time and The Worst Time of your Life! Yes, only because I have experienced it myself, I never would have believed how complex suffering can be. It is where were we can live in 2 parts of our life at the same time. The pain of grief, emptiness and disappointment can be the absolute hardest and darkest time ever experienced. But the emptying out of self, dependency on God during this time of darkness along with the mindset that nothing else matters, can also be the most intimate time we have ever experienced. To be swallowed up by the love and mercy of God, knowing that the "All Knowing" is walking every step with us, is too amazing to articulate.

"There are as many nights as days, and the one is just

as long as the other in the years' course. Even a happy

life cannot be without a measure of darkness, and the

word 'happy would lose its meaning if it were not

balanced by sadness.

Allow it to Take your Trust and Dependency to an Entirely New Level

As humans we have the tendency to want to be our own God. Just like we want to control and drive our own car! Many times, we think we are letting go and allowing God to be in control, but our hands are all over it. Most of us would be totally shocked if we could look into the dark and see our handprints, body prints and thought inputs which influences a situation we thought we had given over to the Father.

The sacrifice to give everything even our thoughts over to Christ is unexplainable without Him. But it is important that we understand that most of our growth comes through our trails and challenges not through our celebrations. It is in the breaking, suffering and the grieving that causes us to be exclusively His. When we get to the place in Christ where we can maintain and grow in this higher level in Him then spiritual maturity begins. We are at a place that many people fail to achieve. We are at a new level of trust, expectation, and responsibility. Our conversations with Him start to increase and become clearer. We start learning God for who He is. Much of what we start learning is from the relationship we develop simply through being personally intimate with Him.

At this level of sanctification, we start understanding the ways of God more. Instead of guessing and questioning, why and how come, we start seeing in our walk how things had to happen the way they did for us to get empty and useable by God. We start understanding the deeper things of God because we start thinking more and more like Him.

Yes, suffering is an emptying out and a releasing but in Christ eyes it is more about the refilling, the renewing, and the remaking of your relationship with Him.

We start understanding that everyone has a different bottom level. Some must go deeper than others depending on their personality, purpose, and resistance to God. We start understanding that oftentimes the grief that we go through *Had to Happen*. Nothing else would have broken us like this specific suffering. We had to get broken open for us to become full. It becomes real when everything had to be taken away from us in order for us to fully trust God. More and more we discover that the suffering was not just for the sake of suffering, it was for us to release what we so tightly held on to and replace it with trust.

Christian Blue Print

Keeping our eyes and mind on Christ is becoming a greater challenge than ever before. Being able to focus on the Father with the increase of world violence, pandemics, poverty and increasing social issues is impossible without the help and guidance of God. But when we see that we have an opportunity to know Him at a higher level let us recognize and take full advantage of it. Let us react quickly, and more urgent than what we are used to. Some of us believe that Christ just leaves us alone all day. That He goes His way, and we go Ours. Well given the signals in my life, I believe that Christ is constantly giving us signs and signals to see him, commune with Him and to include Him in our daily lives. Due to the increase in our world problems, our level of focus must be higher and more solid than ever before. As the world increase in its state of desperation, we must increase in the boldness of concentrating on Him.

As Christian's let us not be casual in our faith. We should not be of the mindset of doing what we have always done and thinking the way we have always thought.

We will find ourselves, God of thinking and believing at the level of faith that has brought us this far, will carry us through. We must be bolder, and more diligent. Let us pray that God will readjust our Christian energy and actions to give us enough focus and stamina to have the strength and faith we need in this complex era of deep turmoil.

MY PERSONAL STORY

As I write this book, flashbacks from my past keep me humbled and fully aware. Losing my mother was the deepest level of suffering I have ever experienced. When I look back, I have no doubt that God was keeping and protecting me every second of the day. He helped me to think and put one foot in front of the other. Because without Him, I would not have been able to do it. I was in the process of dying myself. I had no energy and I had lost my purpose in life. Losing my mother equated to me as losing my best friend, confidant, travel buddy, she was my god here on earth. She understood me and she loved me with every breath she had in her body. Her unselfish love for her family was my anchor and my motivation, which shaped our relationship my entire life.

Although I knew she was dying from cancer, nothing could have prepared me for her actual death. My significant other was my Angel during this difficult time in my life. He walked with me through the difficult loss of both my parents in a two-year time span. However,

I was not prepared for his sudden departure. He was diagnosed with cancer one week after burying my mom. He died one month later. I remember saying Lord "No" this is more than I can bear. Nothing could have prepared me for the questions, emptiness, and the devastating grief, I had to process and experience every minute of my day.

I was on autopilot every day and all the time. I tried to resume my regular scheduled activities. However, I was only present physically but completely checked out emotionally and spiritually. My initial thought was being concerned for me. "What am I going to do?" How can I go on?" Just getting out of the bed everyday took more energy than I had most of the time. I was afraid of mother leaving me. I did not know how to live without her.

My willingness to take a full breath, in and out, helped sanctify my suffering.

In the midst of my suffering, I remember the Holy Spirit telling me to take a breath. A deep inhaling breath in and a long deep exhaling breath out. This process felt as if I was allowing life inside by pain with each inhale and a push of pain out with each exhale. I had been shallow breathing for quite awhile. However, after I allowed myself to continue to take deep breaths, I began to feel more alive and revived. It was like the full breaths was resuscitation to a body in full cardiac arrest. The shedding of grief had begun and the acceptance of my life without them had emerged. *My breath was a response from me to God saying "I will continue to live and yes Father, I know that I still have a reason and a purpose". That breath was the beginning of me learning to acknowledge to God that I knew he was there. I was being delivered and God was lifting me up. My vision was becoming much clearer now. I could finally see more than my fear and loneliness.*

I know that taking a full breath may seem odd and not common to some people. But when my suffering started, I remember the shallow breathing began. I was unconsciously bringing in a little air and letting out just a little air. I had just enough to survive. I was not capable to give to anything or anyone completely. Everything I did I barely could do, even my breathing. Again, I was there physically but completely absent emotionally and spiritually. I was like a zombie who was programmed for what to do next. There was a blockage and a shield over my emotions. I remember wanting to die.

I felt nothing and I felt everything, at the same time.

I remember when my suffering started changing. It took a while, but I started thinking about other things again, the overwhelming feeling of my loss was no longer consuming my ever thought. I still longed for and missed them horribly, but I could tell that I was coming out of my shock phase. I became more aware of my situation and the people around me. I knew that God was lifting me!

My suffering became sanctified when my perspective changed. The shock was releasing its hold on me. I slowly became more present and was becoming more aware of what I was doing.

God started healing and sanctifying my suffering. It was through God that I was able to lose so much and still have plenty to give. My shock was fading more and more each day, and I was grateful.

I was able to think beyond myself and what I had wanted. It no longer stopped me in my tracts. I still missed them and the life we shared together.

I was no longer leaning on my losses, wanting more of them, but I became desperate on needing God more and more. I realized I couldn't do life here on Earth without God's help. Focusing on Him gave me the strength to realize that yes, there is still life and yes, I still have a purpose, even without them.

My sanctified suffering allowed me to live my life despite of what I no longer had. Things became more spiritual than secular. Even now, I still miss my mother every day. But I am no longer in a deep grief state. My longing and unbearable pain is no more. Because I know my mother's spirit is still alive and watches over me. I still feel her presence around me at times. Our spirits will always be connected.

I would have never thought that one full breath could have meant so much. But it was a new beginning for me. I was being reborn without my mother. Taking a full and purposeful breath was an acknowledgment that I trusted God with my life without my mother. It was a reminder to me; it was time to get up and live!

My mother's love taught me to be strong, courageous and purpose filled. Her prayers for me always talked about me doing what I was purposed to do, regardless of my challenges. While I was still grieving, I knew that God prepared me for this time. I knew that I had to get up and wipe my face and start doing what I was meant to do.

FROM CATERPILLAR TO BUTTERFLY

CHP 4

It is impossible to describe the awesomeness of God. Let us not forget that regardless of how hard we try, we can never explain the Glory of our Father enough! There are no words that exist that can properly give Him the honor that He deserves. We are just not equipped to understand the deepness of our God. Even when we try our hardest it is best that we just trust in knowing that God is fully in control.

God is an everyday miracle worker. We have the tendency to see miracles everyday but because they are so common and right in front of us, we just see them as ever day occurrences. Have you ever wondered why God would choose to turn a caterpillar into a beautiful butterfly? We know that God is in control, and He can do anything that He desires. But with this particular miracle is in our face every day, yet we take away the fact that it is a miracle and reduce it to just being interesting or peculiar. Even scientist stray away from answering how this is possible. When you think about the two insects, they could not be any more different from each other. A caterpillar is slow with fuzzy hair and limited access because it is a ground insect. Yet God choose this insect to get transformed into a colorful beautiful butterfly with bright colors and the ability to fly. But regardless, if we understand or not, we do know that a butterfly has greater advantages than a caterpillar. God has decided to upgrade the caterpillar into an insect that can travel through flying. Just like He does with us. God is always trying to transform us into better Christians that will depend on Him more. God has given the butterfly the knowledge to travel and fly to New Mexico, when the weather gets too cold. It can pick up and go where it needs to go. Isn't it interesting that New Mexico is a place where the butterflies desire to go? It is a miracle that God has put this place of refuge in the mind of the butterfly. He put the desire in them and then He gave them knowledge of where to go and how to get there. The butterfly is also one of the most beautiful insects ever created. It is full of color, detail, and beauty.

The remaking of the insect is more beautiful and noticeable than before.

This transformation is something that we can relate to in our life. A caterpillar has everything it needs to live and thrive. It is fully equipped to do what it is meant to do. But God decided that the caterpillar would transform to a more vibrant insect with the ability to soar.

This is like our relationship with God. God gives us the opportunity to be our very best. When we are born, we have everything we needed. He even gives us gifts and abilities so that we are more equipped in this world. Even though we can fully functional the way that we are through our journey we need spiritual revivals and transformations to get closer and trust Him more. It is often in our hardship and challenges that we grow and learn to depend on God more fully. It is God's heart that hungers for us to be the very best that we can. He is constantly giving us the opportunity to be better, more aware, and closer to Him. It reminds me of us, during our suffering. We have a solid reason to grieve, and we are usually full of pain and questions. And while we are grieving, we live with our suffering every day. Praying for relief and deliverance.

God wants to transform us to be greater Christians just like He transform the caterpillar into a beautiful butterfly.

During our season of pain, we have our good days and our bad ones. And just when we thought we were doing better, sometimes our memory and thoughts takes us to a place where our deep pain resides. And we find ourselves starting over and dealing with the deepest part of our pain again.

This part reminds me of the caterpillar when it was growing out of its skin. Four different times, the skin busted wide open because the skin was too tight for the insect to live inside of anymore. A change had to occur cause the caterpillar could no longer fit inside its current skin. It was during the 4th time that the caterpillar changes into a butterfly. The pupa starts forming over the caterpillar instead of the shell. It can take up to 10 to

14 days for the caterpillar to completely transform to a butterfly.

This reminds me of our time of suffering. It takes a while to heal. During our time of grieving, our suffering is a back-and-forth process. Some days are better than others and at times it feels that we are at the beginning of our grieving process all over again. The 4 times the caterpillar was going through its skin busting exercise is very similar to how we suffer. We can go from sadness to grief to fear just like the caterpillar. And then it can take up to 14 days for the caterpillar to go through the process of metamorphosis and then the new body is changed to a brand-new version of itself, which is the butterfly.

So, when we suffer, and we allow sanctification to take place as we hide inside of God's arms for a period of time we begin to change. This is like the caterpillar being hidden inside of the pupa going through the insect transforms. God is fine-tuning our weapons of patience, understanding, faith and holiness. So that when we are finished with our suffering, we can also come out greater than what we were before we started grieving.

We are Here for an Assignment

God takes our calling and purpose very seriously. There is a reason for each one of us to be here and that is what Christ cares about. It's just like the monarch butterfly when the butterfly comes to life, and it mates with another butterfly. They lay their eggs on the milkweed leaf. After they do this, they only live for 2 more weeks and then they die. Because they die after laying their eggs, it seems like their sole purpose is to reproduce and multiply.

Although our life has many facades. We need to remember that just like the butterfly, we are here for a divine purpose. I know that we try to gain the luxuries of what life provides. We thrive to make life as pleasurable as possible. However, when we get so engrossed at having things and getting acceptance by others, we forget that this world is not our home. We start losing the vision that we are all here on assignment. Once we are finished with that assignment, unless God still has a need for us, there is no longer a reason for us to be here on this current Earthly realm.

God's Protection

God protects the butterfly. Although birds and other insects eat insects. The caterpillar and the butterfly are protected. They don't get eaten by other insects because their taste is so bad. The insects and birds of prey will eat around them. But they automatically know that they will not like their flavor, so they pass them by. This reminds me of how the Father protects us during our suffering. I can only imagine the protection that God gives to us. The things that we are aware of and the things we are not aware of. If God goes out of the way to protect the life of a caterpillar, I can't imagine how far He will go to protect us. This is something that we will never directly know the answer to because we are unaware of what is happening in the spirit realm. Thus, we should rest in the knowing that God is protecting us in ways in which we will never know. Even when we are going through our deep time of suffering, regardless of how much pain and grief we go through we need to thank God in advance that our pain is not greater and deeper than what it is. We have no idea where the level of our pain would be if God was not giving us His grace and mercy, reminding us of who we are in Him, and bringing the right people in our lives, at the perfect time. Regardless of the level of our pain, God is giving us favor and working on our behalf for an early deliverance. As Christians let us not forget that when we hurt, Christ hurts also. In our suffering although we may feel isolated, God is stopping other targets from hurting us. We may not see it, but we need to assume God is fighting for us in the spirit realm. Just like Christ protects the caterpillar and the butterfly by not allowing insects to eat them, He is steadily working behind the scenes to keep us alive and functioning too!

THE BODY, SOUL & SPIRIT

CHP 5

Grief opens a place in our hearts,

that we never knew could hurt so profoundly,

But it also opens this same place to a love,

we never imagined possible."

Listen closely, "We are made in God's image!!!" When you really think about "the image of God" it is indescribable that God would make us like Him. God could have made us in any image. We would not have known the difference. But to know that He loves us so intense that He made us like himself, is beyond understanding and words. Just think, He knew that Adam and Eve would betray Him. He also knew we would be a self-centered, evil, idol-worshipping people who would steadily look for other things and idols to worship, instead of Him. Knowing all of this, God still gave us His best, which was Himself!

Our body is the body of Christ. Although the body is what we are the most consumed with, the one we understand the most, yet we still are wayward in our thinking, we often miss what Christ is trying to accomplish. The body is where we are housed inside of. It is our protective covering here on earth, but without the soul and the spirit, it has no meaning. It is only an outward shell.

As humans, we usually judge others totally on what we see. We have made the body a major focal point. It is a big part of who we are, we get consumed with making it more enticing and eye catching to others rather than being holy before Christ. We often forget that we will be transformed. The body as we know it will be gone. Now let me explain, the body is very important because it houses every part of us (Soul & Spirit). We have made a grave mistake to look at the body and allow what we see to conclude judgment about a person. We give it too much attention and then we forget that as humans we have a spirit and a soul too. I know that it would take a big adjustment to look at each person and not notice their body but instead focus on their spirit.–Usually when we get to know someone, we are getting to know their spirit. Their personality is the first thing we see. The spirit is their motivation, perspective, it is demonstrated in how they live their life. It is also how they connect to others and their level of empathy and concern.

God is very clear that our body is a temple for Him to live. He puts a lot of emphasis on how we need to take care of our temples, so that we can be prepared to do our calling.

1 Corinthians 6:19-20 says, *"Do you not know that your bodies are temples of the Holy Spirit, who is in you, whom you have received from God? You are not your own; you were bought at a price. Therefore, honor God with your bodies."*

In the verse above, it is clear that God leaves the care of our body as our own personal responsibility. Our power to control our own body is talked about much differently than our spirit and soul.

We don't usually see a person's personality as their spirit, but it is. You may have heard someone say "Oh, I don't like her spirit, she is rude." The spirit is most often what you see and hear when a person first opens their mouth.

This includes their will, emotions, and personal character.

This is something we should not ignore. Our spirit needs to be monitored and checked frequently to make sure we are modeling after Christ.

We hear about the word soul repeatedly. And at times, the word soul and spirit are used in the same context. (Many experts believe that they are one and the same). But the soul is looked at as being deeper and more complex, it is our entire being. The Bible says that the soul still exists after the physical body is gone. It emphasizes the importance of the soul's relationship with God and the need for spiritual redemption and salvation. In general, the soul is often understood as the eternal and immaterial aspect of a person, which is unique and separates them from other living creatures. *Oftentimes the spirit and the soul are so similar, only the Holy Spirit can discern between them.*

1 Thessalonians 5:23 states: "Now may the God of peace himself sanctify you completely and may your whole spirit and soul and body be kept blameless at the coming of our Lord Jesus Christ." **This verse suggests that we are made up of three distinct parts: spirit, soul, and body.**

1 Thessalonians 5:23 encourages believers to be sanctified completely, spirit, soul, and body.

Hebrews 4:12: "For the word of God is living and active, sharper than any two-edged sword, piercing to the division of soul and of spirit, of joints and of marrow, and discerning the thoughts and intentions of the heart." **This verse suggests that the soul and spirit can be distinguished from one another.**

Matthew 10:28: "And do not fear those who kill the body but cannot kill the soul. Rather fear him who can destroy both soul and body in hell." **This verse implies that the soul is separate from the body and continues to exist even after death.**

Mark 8:36-37: "For what does it profit a man to gain the whole world and forfeit his soul? For what can a man give in return for his soul?"

The Christian Blue Print

As Christians, we can become so forgetful and so self-centered when it comes to the grace of God and what He continuously does for us. Some of us go from intense focus to casual focus as it relates to what we want. Many of us are intense when we are asking God for help but too casual when we start living out our life day to day.

It is dangerous to be too casual about the things of God. We should be awake and always prepared to help, pray, and lift others. When we ask God for healing and restoration, he expects us to be willing to live out the lifestyle that honors that healing. It is not fair for us to get what we need from God, mutter a quick thank you and start life again with no spiritual assessment. Now we know that whatever Christ does it is excellent and complete. But many of us will receive our deliverance and then immediately continue the habits that got us into a rut in the first place.

The Pain will Leave Once it has Finished Teaching You!

This is also true when we need rescuing from our suffering.

It is important for us to realize that when we are healed from our grief and suffering, God customizes our healing specifically for each individual person. He looks at our spirit and soul and then gives us just what we need and does a complete restoration.

For those of you who doubt that God deals with us this specific and customized, listen closely. He would not give Tonya the healing that Diane needs. And He is not going to extend Franks understanding if he does not need it at this time. Each healing is specific to who we are, what we are going through and our relationship with Him. He also looks at our past experiences, what we have been healed from and what we still need to receive healing from. Whenever God rescues us from any situation, he equips us to have the ultimate healing. Unfortunately, as humans, after the newness of our healing wears off, we start getting distracted by our everyday responsibilities again, we tend to forget the graciousness of God. We go back to the habits we have been accustomed to. After a while, we don't stop considering the amazing and strategic healing process the Father blessed us with. We just start casually living in our healing. What I am saying is that after every deliverance we need to assess and make sure we are not inviting things and people in our life that challenge and work against the healing that the Father has done. We must stay guarded and focused on what Christ has done. We need to work on our behavior and decisions and make sure they align with the healing that has happened. If God heals us and we go right back to negative talk, non-faith thinking, and hanging around those who don't believe that each of us have a purpose, our healing will become watered down and less and less effective. Please understand that it is not that God's healing can disappear, but whatever you give the most energy to is your God for that day. **So, if you are allowing negativity, dangerous thinking people and a lack of faith to consume your thoughts, then that is what will consume your spirit! Not your healing, but whatever you give your most energy too!**

After we seek God for help and healing, we must do our part to ensure that our behavior and decisions feed and nurture the healing we have been given.

TRANSFORMATION LEADS TO SELF DISCOVERY

CHP 6

We tend to normalize the things of God so that we can understand them. We bring them down to us, in our minimum understanding, instead of us going higher and higher to reach them.

The more you transform and elevate higher in God, the more you will automatically discover more about you and why you do the things that you do! The more curious you are, the more you will discover. This book talks a lot about transformation and moving higher and higher in God. We give examples of how our change is similar to the caterpillar transforming to a butterfly, how to sanctify your suffering in the midst of suffering, how to stay in a place of healing and deliverance while living in a world of overwhelming chaos, violence and the unknown.

One of the most natural ways for us to transform to another level in God is through our gifts and purpose.

Knowing that each of us was born and gifted with our own special calling and purpose is powerful! Knowing that it is not anything we can work or try to obtain; but this gift has been in us since the day we were born, it's beyond incredible! Although some of us are curious, as Christians we are simply not as confident in what our purpose and gifts are to move boldly in them. We are ill-equipped because we lack understanding and proper teaching in this area. Therefore, we lack in the strength, power, and influence that God wants us to have. Most of us would like to delve into our gifts and purpose more but due to the many challenges and distractions we experience every day, our calling and purpose is not in our top 3 most important things. Many of us struggle just to keep our faith daily.

As Christians we know that we have gifts. We have downplayed the entire subject about gifts and purpose. It seems-as though the idea of gifts goes in and out of our thoughts. Sometimes it is loud and then soft again. There might be a time when everyone is talking about it and then you don't hear about it anymore. We have not fully grabbed on to the idea of living a life totally immersed in our gifts. We tend to talk and acknowledge the idea of having a purpose instead. This is good, but the Father has designed us so that our gifts work directly with our purpose. *He gave us the gifts that we have, so that our purpose can be more successful. They work hand in hand.*

It is extraordinary and phenomenal that God has graced us with special gifts in addition to the favor He already gives to us. However, as a society, we get more thrills with Superman and other cartoons characters with fake superpowers. Compared to marvel comics, we can't shoot out fire from our mouth, or fly from one dimension to the next, but when used properly, our gifts are powerfully impressive also!

One of the reasons why we are not extra excited about our gifts is because, we see our gifts as being common to what we already can do. For those with the gift of discernment, or the gift of teaching, although the gifts are interesting, we are not impressed with someone who can teach well. Nor with someone that is discerning and knows things. We tend to normalize the things of God to understand them. We bring them down to us, with a minimum understanding, instead of us going higher and higher to reach them.

As Christians, we have toned down our gifts to the point that we don't even see them as a real advantage. We don't emphasize our gifting or even talk about them. So, we don't purposefully use our gifts in our daily life because many of us don't know what we are gifted in, and because we don't look at our gifts as a big deal. We desire to fit in and not stand out, we do what other people do. We would be surprised how much we try to keep ourselves balanced with the people around us. If the majority don't see their gifts as a miracle and an obvious gift from God, then in most cases, the minority will not either.

The Enemies Scheme Against You!

The enemy is constantly watching us. He has a special interest in what we like and want we don't like. There is special attention towards our weaknesses and our vulnerabilities. He is also interested in the strength of our faith and the foundation around us. He started strategizing a plan for us when we were babies. Our support system is closely looked at. The enemy looks at the strength of faith you were raised in and the people in your inner circle that are strong Christians that might ruin his plan!!!

The enemy knows that God has put into all of us abilities, gifts, and extra proficiencies to have an advantage over society as we live here on earth. God also added a desire in all of us to want to have meaning and purpose. He states that He put our gifts in us while we were still in our mother's womb. Therefore, once we were born, we were already gifted. Although most people don't remember, many of us start acting in our gifts and purpose when we are very young. For example, as parents, we can notice very early if our newborn is strong-willed are not. They will cry until they get what they want and at 8 months it seems like they are already competing with your power! As parents, we don't realize that they are simply being "who they are". We have no idea that their gifts are already being used in their small personalities. The baby grows and grows until she is a confident little girl. We can easily see her personality at 4 years old. Now that she can talk and has some understanding she tends to be bossy, no-nonsense, and very clear about what she wants and doesn't want. She is a natural born leader, in charge and making things happen. Her parents sometimes giggles because she is such a handful, but other times they discipline her for being so demanding.

Without knowing it, she is already walking in her leadership gift at age 4! The enemy has a plan to make her leadership gift become a communication problem and misunderstanding for the rest of her life. When she starts going to school and caring about friendships, her bossiness starts to become a real issue. The very thing she is gifted in, is what brings her the most problems. Other kids don't want to play with her because they are afraid of her and don't like being bossed around. Although she naturally can control and give direction, at times, she will sit back and not say anything due to being afraid of being ridiculed for this gift inside her. As she grows, her leadership abilities never leave her, but she has learned to become cautious about what she says and tries not to be confrontational. Her ability to lead has caused her problems and confrontations with others. She begins to resent this gift within her. She is always confronted by what she says or how she says it. As her world becomes busier, she finds that she has become a master at hiding the leader within, so she is not targeted as being mean!

Because we are not that knowledgeable about gifts and how they form, she is never taught how to be patient with others and how to address people with love and respect first. So, her gift is often received as harsh, self-centered, and arrogant. She battles on and off for the rest of her life with her boldness. She never quite understood her gift in leadership. Her God-given blessing has been twisted into a communication curse the enemy plotted when she was born.

The enemies plan worked. She will never live fully in her boldness and gift. She never was taught to love people first before directing them. She never reached the level of humbleness that she needed, to be direct and connecting at the same time. She tried but she never fully gave this part of her life over to Christ so that He could teach and direct her. So, she remained bold and sometimes it was fine but at other times it caused misunderstandings. It brought problems to her professional life. Even in her intimate relationships, she always seemed much stronger and more motivated than her mate. She would find herself being impatient and wanting someone with a bolder personality that could speak up when needed. She wondered if she would ever find someone that had a strong and solid persona also. She was tired of being more manly than her man!! In her relationships, she found that in most cases, he was scared of her, and she did not respect him.

She had the ability to lead but because of the problems it brought she spent most of her time getting out of mess and conflict instead of walking boldly in her purpose. Her gift never got close to the level that Christ purposed for her life.

So often the things that we are gifted in, is also what others don't understand about us. Our purpose begins in us as little children, as life continues, the challenge of real life becomes more and more overwhelming. Many times, due to our busy schedules the idea of mastering our purpose becomes less and less important. Our gifts just slide so easily into our personality, many of us don't see our enhanced ability as a real gift from God. Although we live with this every day, many of us, don't see our ability as a real advantage. We just allow it to blend in with the rest of our personality, it becomes less and less valuable to us. Oftentimes, it is much later in life when our kids are grown and life slows down, that we start re-asking again, "What are my gifts and what is my purpose"?

Discovering a New Godly Peace, Joy & Freedom

When we start seeing ourselves as gifted, anointed, and only here to fulfill an assignment, we are at a new level with God. Everything and everyone are different. Being able to internalize every day, "I am only here for an assignment" gives us greater purpose and keeps us balanced.

When we get the understanding deep in our spirit, what mission we are to fulfill here on earth. Our attitude about life and others completely changes. Our peace, joy and freedom are new and different because we don't allow unimportant things to distract us from God. It is much easier knowing who is important and who is not, when you know you are here on assignment. Chaos does not have power over you because you no longer have time to internalize the mess that comes with the chaos.

As Christians, we really need to understand that God wants us happy and excited about life. He loves us and when we hurt, He hurts. Although, He wants the very best for us, He did not create us to be happy. As Christians, we are here to make a difference.

If we can find happiness along the way that is great! His promises about joy, freedom and peace will be completely fulfilled in heaven.

But most of us live our life like there is nothing else that we are hoping for. Everything that we want, have or desire is here on earth. We allow ourselves to get distracted from God into this chaos here on Earth. We end up getting swallowed up by the problems and the challenges of this world, just like the enemy wants. We get distracted and start losing site of why we are here. We start living in this world, like there is no other reason for us to be here, and we never fully execute the power that we have inside.

(SUFFERING)

This happens during our time of grief also. Losing someone and going through all the things that are grief-worthy, would be very different if we saw ourselves as being on assignment and the person that we are grieving for is on assignment, too. Now I am not saying we would never be hurt but I am saying that if we saw living here on Earth as a temporary stay for us to accomplish our task, then this need to hold on to what we have and never let go, would not have the power that it presently possesses.

When we communicate with God as someone, who is clear about their assignment and reason, God can then connect with us in a new way! We then are at a new level with Him. We are finally able to see life as God sees it! Our distractions, dangerous chaos, and the ups and downs challenges of everyday life, no longer has power over us because our focus is solely on our assignment. Having the power to ignore common distractions and not worrying about who likes you and who doesn't is a new free way of living for most of us. What I am saying is, when you see yourself as a person here for a mission, you are physically present but absent most of the time both emotionally and spiritually.

Christian Blueprint

Regardless of how gifted we are, God is not going to make us pursue our purpose. He is not going to pump us up every few days with a high euphoric longing for us to live out our calling. He has already put the desire in us when He gifted us.

He wants us to have faith and trust Him when it comes to our calling. Regardless of how we feel, or how impossible it appears, He wants us to believe with no doubt, that what He promised will come to pass.

Everything about God is a choice. He allows us to decide if we believe, how much we will believe, and how much energy and loyalty we put into the things that we believe in. He allows us to have free range. In many cases, God would allow us to take our purpose as high as we have the mindset to do so. If we pray for it, and work for it, God will allow us to have it.

During your time of suffering, allows yourself the time to remember that you are gifted and have purpose. Reminding yourself over and over that God expects our life to be full of meaning and reason. He gives you a healthy balance during your grief. Seeing yourself this way, allows you to remember that even though you are still grieving your purpose and destiny is awaiting you to continue your journey which was created just for you.

SANCTIFY YOUR WEAPONS!

CHP 7

When we think about Godly weapons, we assume that they are all sufficient, ready to be used and that no additional work is needed! But let's be real, what will work for one person may not work at all for someone else.

*As you go through your grieving process, all the weapons can be helpful. Depending on the level of your suffering, several may need to be used at the same time. We need to understand that Godly weapons are different from earthly weapons. They are not only weapons that you can use against demonic forces, but they are weapons you can use against suffering, depression, lack of faith, etc. The weapons are created for believers in Christ It builds you up to be able to forgive, think more positively, and not be overwhelmed with negativity.

The power of the weapons depends on the faith of the person using them!

Let me be clear, everything the Father gives us is perfect and needs no adjustment. However, depending on how we use what has been given determines how effective it is. It simply is not enough to take the weapons with minimal faith, inadequate expectations, and assume because we have a spiritual weapon that it will work to full capability. Let me be clear, all the weapons that the Father gives us have supernatural power because it comes from the heavenly realm and not the earthly realm. However, they still can't work on their own. Its effectiveness will always depend on the strength, courage and the faith of the person using it. Many times, we forget that we also have a responsibility as we prepare ourselves to use God's weapons.

Let's admit it, we have mastered how to take full advantage of God's goodness and grace. As Christians, we know He is good, but many of us have never internalized the true goodness of our faithful and perfect God. Yes, we are limited to what we can consume and understand. But many of us don't even try. We have become just too comfortable at basking in his promises every day and forgetting to thank Him for the seen and unseen dangers that He guards us from every second of every day. I truly believe that when we finally see Christ, and we see all his Glory we will be instantly filled with overwhelming fear, shame, and shock. Every one of us will instantly regret that we did not surrender more, give more, and love Him so much more! His presence will overwhelm us to the point that the only thing we will be able to say is Holy Holy Holy!

Every night, we make the assumption that we will wake up to a brand-new day casually and boldly believing it just has to be. Never wondering what it would be like if the next day never came. Completely overlooking the fact that the King of Everything and Everyone is perfectly committed to giving us new days, with different temperatures and time zones, all over the world, just for us. He does not have to do it or give it, but He chooses to, regardless of our faithfulness towards Him.

If we look back, we talked about how we de-emphasize our purpose and gifts in the previous chapter. We tend to do the same thing with the spiritual weapons He has given. While we tend to use some of the weapons more than others, we need to take seriously their effectiveness and intended power. Weapons with faith gives us an upper edge on anything that we might be going through.

Here are some examples:

Meditation – the Thought Regulator

Some of us as Christians are weary about meditation because we are afraid that it is weird, New Age and an ungodly practice.

Meditation does not control you; you control it. It has no power unless you give it power. And it is not ungodly unless you make it ungodly.

But it can be very powerful when you are able to stop emotional distractions and other useless thoughts from seeping in your thought life. Meditation is a calming practice to get your thoughts exactly where you want them.

It usually involves going to a quiet place and focusing on where you want your mind to be. You can focus and then say an affirmation repeatedly. If it is during a time of suffering, you can repeat affirmations like: "This too shall pass" or "God will never leave me". The practice of meditation has been found to have numerous benefits for mental, emotional, and physical well-being. It can also help reduce stress, improve concentration and memory, enhance self-awareness, promote emotional balance, increase relaxation, and foster a sense of inner peace and clarity.

WARNING: *Don't erase prayer for meditation. Prayer is direct communication with God, it serves an entirely different purpose. With meditation, you can put your mind where you want it to go. You can be a non-believer and meditate every day. But prayer is a 1:1 link to the Father. Your focus and every part of yourself should be totally submitted to God while you talk to Him. With prayer you are not seeking calmness or just to clear your mind with good thoughts. It is a time that you are focused and communicating with your eternal Father.

Prayer – can be the most effective weapon

Many Christians believe that prayer is the most dangerous weapon that God has given. So therefore, prayer during your grieving stage is vital. It is amazing that through prayer we can request what we need, give thanks and praise, ask for forgiveness, or just talk about everyday life issues. God is always reachable through prayer. The more you pray the more dangerous your prayers become.

Unlike meditation the more you **pray,** the closer you tend to be with Christ. **Your prayer life** can develop **into** a constantly talking to God all day and every day. The build-up of all that **prayer increases** your relationship with Him. **The** stronger your relationship, the more you learn how to ask, what to ask for, and how God deals with you specifically.

To get to the place where you can constantly talk with God despite your many life distractions is powerful. It develops a quick character-builder, spiritual strength and a consciousness sensitive to what the Holy Spirit is saying.

Beware, because the most effective prayer is when you are so focused on what you are doing, you envision yourself talking and having a conversation with the Father during the process. You began to live at a point where you are talking to God like He is your very best friend. Honoring Him with submissiveness as your Father and King. Not always asking for something, but a real live conversation talking about expectations, choices, and life in general.

How to Strengthen your Prayers.

- Focus, focus and more focus. God wants your direct and full attention. He wants us to be able to stop eating, turn off the TV and cease from using our cell phone, while talking with Him. He demands our sincere focus, pushing all distractions and all other thoughts completely aside. Although this may seem impossible, it can be done, quickly and successfully. It is easy to be praying to God but thinking about something else! As Christians, let's learn to give 100% of our attention to God. It is the very least we should do. Some people need to meditate and gather their thoughts before seeking God in prayer. This allows for an incredible connection and focus.

- Learn to talk to Him all the time. Let me be clear, I am talking about all day and all the time. Learn to master how to talk to Him without expecting a response. Just involve Him in your everyday activities. Conversate with Him, just like you would a best friend. This is where your prayers are at a deeper level and effectiveness. God wants us to include Him in everything.

Journaling – the ability to recall experiences

Writing your thoughts down is not for everyone. And yet, there are those who can jot down their thoughts more accurately than they can speak to them. What I am saying is that writing either works for you or it doesn't. It can be beautiful and a very powerful experience when you can keep a book that you wrote in about break throughs, thoughts, ideas, gratitude or even answers from God. When you can create a place where you can go back and re-read what was on your mind or an experience you had, it can be amazing.

The experienced journalist understands how powerful it can be to go back 5 years and read your live words and feelings, just like you are re-living the experience again.

Journaling is not about today, it is about being able to recapture your past, in the future.

Please remember there are decisions that need to be made when you decide to make journaling apart of your spiritual journey. You need to decide if your journal is private? And at what level of privacy. Everyone is different but most journals are completely off limits from other people. It is often kept in a private place. Because it is common to write thoughts and experiences that are private and important to examine at what level is needed to guard your book. Should your finished journal be under lock and key? Or just keeping it under some sweaters in your closet?

Please be aware the more you try to keep your special book hidden, the more interested others will be to read it. The more hush-hush you are about it; the more others will be tempted to look through it. Despite whom you are or how exciting your life is, you have secrets, those closest to you want to know about them also!

WARNING – As you work to keep your journaling sanctified, you must understand that the level of the specialness and value of your journal, greatly depends on the honesty and integrity that you had while you were writing. If you are writing and your thoughts are somewhere else, or if you are writing just because you promised yourself you would write every single Monday then this exercise is useless!! The lack of reason and commitment that you have as you are journaling, will be the same "so who cares" perspective when you go back to read it.

*Most journals lack in meaning and purpose when you write simply because you told yourself to. Just remember that journaling is supposed to be a special, sacred, and private thing, and the more you remember this, the more valuable your journal will be in the future.

Giving –Don't get it twisted; 10% is the least we should be giving!

Every person living, has experienced the awesome, non-ending love of our Father every single day. We breathe, walk, and enjoy the beauty of each day, with no thought of saying thank you or surrendering more to him. The whole idea of giving is no stranger to Christians. We know the advice to give a minimum of 10% tithe is something that most of us have heard over and over. As much as it has been drilled in us, many of us have conditioned ourselves to give it, faithfully. The Bible talks about giving and helping others. Many of us base how serious we are in your relationship with God, on our giving history. We allow our tithe record to determine our relationship with God.

Although we tend to see things from one perspective, Christ doesn't. Yes! We should tithe our money. But what Christ wants from us is to be generous givers, just like He is!

WARNING: Sanctify your giving by not just looking at tithe and the money aspect, but instead look at the entire fullness of who you are and where your heart is. You can be a faithful tithe giver and still not love people. Some people see their giving history as an example of how much they are committed. To give money twice a month is no big deal for some. Yet the same people that don't mind giving, can have a very serious problem forgiving and/or not holding a grudge! God wants us to be a giver of all things. He wants us to model after Him when it comes to our mindset of giving. God wants us to be a giver of time, givers of our energy, and generous in how we think. He wants us to be filled with the joy of blessing others. Now don't get it twisted, He does not want us to over give just to give. We need to make sure that our giving is thoughtful and wise. But He really desires for us to have more joy giving than receiving. Thinking of ourselves last and not first, when it comes to giving is how you sanctify it.

Fasting – a private and personal sacrifice to God.

Many people look at fasting as a tradition that is only done by the most committed and the most serious. This is not necessarily true but fasting is a sacrifice and often one of the harder weapons to maintain success. Although the process may be difficult, many Christians receive great strength and direction from it. It is common for most of us to be first acquainted to fasting through the church we attend. Although you can fast for any reason, sometimes churches will fast during special times such as, at the beginning of a new year for protection, guidance, and favor. Our introduction usually starts in the church but when we become more mature in Christ we will then fast for our own specific reasons and convictions.

To sanctify your fast and use it as a weapon, you must stop doing something that you like or usually do, and then fill the extra time communicating and focusing on Christ. Many people use food, as a sacrifice. Some might skip breakfast and lunch for a week and only eat dinner. Others will decide to only drink liquids instead of eating food for a set amount of time. Therefore, the time normally used to ear or prepare food would now be the extra time to communicate and spend time with God. Many people expect to hear from God for clarity during this special time of prayer and fasting.

The beauty of this weapon is that it allows you to get more open and sensitive to what Christ is saying to you. Your willingness to sacrifice is not an easy task and usually not something most people want to do. However, fasting keeps you more aware and it positions you to hear Christ more accurately.

The more that we take out of our daily life, the more Christ we can put in!

Please be aware that people sacrifice many things, such as: smoking cigarettes, watching television, or even drinking soda. God is not as concerned about what we give up as He is about us sacrificing with full intentions to connect with Him more. He wants us to be willing to let go of our normal routine and make Him the priority that He deserves to be.

Unless you are conditioned to fast. Many people fast as a last resort for spiritual direction. This is not usually the first weapon we think of. For many it is the last option we do when we are desperate to hear from God.

WARNING: Sanctify your fasting by keeping it private and personal. An intimate sacrifice to God is both precious and very sacred. It means a lot to God that we are willing to give up something that we love to get closer to Him. So let your commitment to sacrifice be between you and the Father only. The Bible talks about how the Pharisees would fast and then walk up and down the streets looking distraught, hungry, and desperate. They would tell whoever they could find they were going without food. The Pharisees did this to get sympathy and extra attention from others and to be seen as ultra-religious.

Fasting is a strong way to increase your commitment to Christ when it is done with the right intentions. The Bible says, if we must tell everyone about our sacrifice to get extra attention from others, the pity they give to us, is all the reward we will receive!

Matthew 6:16-17 NIV

16 When you fast, do not look somber as the hypocrites do, for they disfigure their faces to show others they are fasting. Truly I tell you, they have received their reward in full. 17 But when you fast, put oil on your head and wash your face, 18 so that it will not be obvious to others that you are fasting, but only to your Father who is unseen; and your Father, who sees what is done in secret, will reward you.

Our society is two-faced when it comes to the things of Christ. Many people don't want any association with the word of God, but they are quick to use not only spiritual principles but also spiritual language in their everyday word usage to appear as if they were committed believers. If you just listen to others in our society, many people will call anything associated with "not eating" as a fast. We make a gruesome mistake at casually using the word "fast" when it has nothing to do with God or our commitment to Him. Even for medical reasons, doctors will use the word "fast" to tell us not to eat food before a procedure.

Now this has not been widely discussed. But using this spiritual word to define trying to lose weight or for reasons not associated by God, takes away the beautiful sacramental 1:1 time God designed it to be.

The Word of God   - our physical weapon and our guide here on earth.

Being able to recite the word of God, by memory, brings great advantage and ongoing comfort and confidence. Once you know "the word" it can never be taken from you. *When you are so familiar with the word of God, that you can quote verses from the Bible as a weapon and a hard stance against whatever you are going through. The invisible spiritual warfare is invoked when you use this tactic in your situation.* The Bible is the number one resource which has taught us what we know about God. Without this resource, we would have no knowledge of salvation. The Bible focuses on His life and provides us with guidance on how to live our life. It lays out clearly who God is and what He expects from us people as we serve Him. It is an amazing gift given to us regarding the past, present and future.

All our spiritual comeback and convictions come from the word of God. Everything that we have learned about having a successful Christian life has been from the Word of God. -Although most of us has never thought about it this way, without the Bible instructing us and explaining God's Plan to us, we would be in complete chaos, trying to fight this incredible battle on our own.

WARNING: After hearing the same stories year after year and from childhood to adulthood it is easy to start taking the word of God for granted. Our society has become impatient and unappreciative. Some have become bored with the Bible and curious about the latest faith trends out there. So instead of searching the scriptures ourselves and separating the truth from the fiction, many people will go and commit to the spiritual trends that are seen as a status symbol especially if it is popular.

Many of us remember in the 1960's and 70's when the New Age religion re-emerged. The roots go as far back as the Theosophy and the New Thought Movement in the 19th.

century. This movement has combined the spiritual and metaphysical beliefs that suggest that we are all whole, despite how tore down we may be. Many religions has spiraled from this "anything goes" ideology of New Age that supports more self-glory than God glory. This teaching takes away God and still offers prosperity, peace and wholeness tends, to attract large groups. *As humans we are attracted to a religion that tends to elevate our own self and claims that we have power to be our own God.*

Although there are various religions and sects emerging at a speed we could never count, Scientology is another popular religion that has gotten the attention of the media. There has been people that has criticized this belief publicly. But it has not slowed down the public interest. It is presented as just another option to live by. Just like New Age this belief tends to water down the Gospel as being part of other religions that can't be proven. Let's be real, almost all religions, good and bad, support faith, wholeness, and kindness. They steal many of their principals from the WORD OF GOD but DON'T want a relationship with God.

Scientology is another sect that offers courses and teachings to followers to reinforce a committed lifestyle. It does not support an official doctrine regarding the existence of God. Instead, it focuses on the nature of an individuals' mind, spirit, and personal journey towards self - improvement and spiritual enlightenment. It also incorporates self-help, psychology, and other spiritual practices. Although it has been controversial it has many followers worldwide. *It is interesting how many humans feel a deep need to follow or strongly believe in some form of human goodness and ethics.* And if the movement stresses self-growth, a sense of faith and human decency the vast number of people will often be at least curious. Too many people are willing to replace "being good" with "being with God." Being involved with Scientology is a status. Many see this as the wealthy and progressive religion because there are known celebrities that are members. People want to be where the "cool, beautiful and famous" people are!

As Christians we need to stay abnormally cautious. Without being paranoid, we need to be ultra-sensitive to what we see, say, and invite in our lives. Depending on your gifts you might be attracted to people and things that are "almost" God but are planted to harm you. Please understand that the closer you are to Christ the more strategic and angrier the enemy is. He is a master at creating replicas of what is holy. Unless you must remain prayed up, sensitive to the Holy Ghost, and focus on your assignment, even as a Christian you will be tricked!!

It is a constant battle every day for us not to sway by the noise of the world. Even when we have experienced God, due to our curiosity and the work of the enemy it is a second-by-second warfare that is hovering over us. It is customized to expose our weaknesses and tempt us with the things we want best. We need to stay on guard and realize that the enemy is constantly trying to keep us distracted from God. That is why so many Christians go back and forth and on and off when it comes to our commitment.

Sanctify your relationship by not being influenced by the constant noise and movement of the world, but step to the world of God and allow the Father to guide your movements. Don't allow looking for the "next best thing" in your life to sway your relationship with God. Now don't get me wrong, we should always want to get closer and bigger in Christ. But don't allow the noise of the world to cause you to move faster than the speed God is moving in. Although we want more and more, always allow there to be a sense of satisfaction with the Father, as you wait for your next step in Him.

We need to realize that the magic that lays on every single page of the Bible starts fading off and losing its uniqueness if we don't stay prayerful and build our relationship with Him. Too many of us become comfortable in our present level of relationship and don't work on growing in Him. The more dangerous and violent the world gets, the more we need to increase in our faith. It's interesting the commitment we have at going to the gym and working out our bodies every day. But as life continues, we need to increase our time with God and expound on our understanding of Him more. Again, if we could only get a sneak peek of the invisible second-by-second spiritual fight that is happening around us then where is our faith, as this approach causes us to doubt.

Sanctify the word of God by allowing its old history to help justify your faith. Don't allow the oldness of the gospel to bore you. Don't let the age of the Word of God make you feel that it is no longer relevant. Instead allow the history of it to help justify the power of it and the reason why it is the greatest spiritual force in the world!!! Let it speak to you and give you answers for how and why we were made and how things began. Stay guarded and pray that God will make you fall in love with the word and gain a never before excitement for it. Ask Him to refresh your interest, clarity, and perspective for the word of God. Don't expose yourself to the different trends and the new religions of society. Stay far from it and don't allow yourself to be curious. In fact, make the idea of other religions something you hate and have no tolerance for. It is important to prepare your mind there will be many beliefs that will borrow concepts and ideology from the Word of God, but it is not really God. Sanctify your Bible knowledge asking Him to allow you not to be distracted by the "new things" constantly being offered by the world.

Suffering - During your time of great suffering and grieving read the word more than what you usually do. It is also a good time to memorize verses that speaks directly to what you are going through. Study the life on Job and allow his sufferings to minister to you.

Listen closely, if you are already suffering, the enemy will use your natural pain and greatly increase it by 100-fold! As much pain as you might be in, the enemy will play and distort your emotions resulting in keeping you from praying, reading and even talking to God. The very things you need for comfort, the enemy will make them hard to reach. But whatever you do, fight your way through. Don't allow your feelings of "I don't feel like it" to distract you from what is available to you. Remember as you grieve, envision yourself in the future walking completely in your purpose. See yourself mastering your gifts. Re-establish this in yourself despite your suffering. You are still fully alive, and God has a customized plan just for you. In despite of knowing the answers to the suffering, God knows best and there is a reason He has allowed it. Your suffering and the deliverance from it, plays an extremely large part to your present and future self.

*Despite how you feel and what you see, trust that He knows the future and He is shaping your life to walk boldly in His customized plan for you!

ALWAYS LOOKING FOR THE "NEXT THING"

In a world of endless wonder,

Where boredom spreads like thunder,

We find ourselves forever seeking,

Always looking, never peaking.

For we are creatures born to roam,

Restless souls, never feeling home,

Never satisfied, always yearning,

For the next adventure, for the next learning.

We tire swiftly of what once enthralled,

As boredom's chains are tightly installed,

Novelty fades, excitement wanes,

Leaving us empty, seeking new plains.

The gadgets, the gadgets, they come and go,

With each new release, our fascination grows,

But oh, how quickly they lose their allure,

As we search for something more, something pure.

We crave the thrill of the unexplored,

The mystery of the yet restored,

In restless hearts, the craving thrives,

For the next big thing that ignites our lives.

No stone is left unturned, no path untraveled,

As we push our limits, our souls unraveled,

We yearn for novelty, for change and surprise,

As boredom's grip tightens, it's no surprise.

But in this endless quest to escape the mundane,

Do we miss the beauty of the terrain?

Do we lose sight of the treasures near,

In our pursuit of what's far and unclear?

For life is filled with moments divine,

Tiny miracles that oft we decline,

In our constant chase for what's yet to come,

Leaving behind what's already begun.

So let us pause, let us take a breath,

And savor the simple, forget the rest,

For in the quiet stillness, we just might see,

The joy and contentment we claim to seek.

In this cycle of chasing and craving,

In this never-ending game we're playing,

May we find solace in the present hour,

And realize that true fulfillment is within our power.

For life's grandest wonders lie not afar,

But in the joy of being, wherever we are,

So let us embrace the beauty of here and now,

And find the peace that only stillness can endow.

SANCTIFIED PREPARATION FOR A VICTORIOUS LIFE ON EARTH

CHP 8

The word "preparation" is not respected much in the life of a Christian. We see what we do more like a task that just need to be done or a way to get closer to God. But we rarely look at what we do as a preparation for our future! But when you think about the pattern of God, everything He does, has to do with our future and the plans He has for us.

We go through teaching now, to prepare us for our amazing future.

The reason He allows us to suffer, is so that we will be strong and able to endure our assignment in the future. Often the reason he allows death to come to our loved ones, because He knows that you need to start over in a place of being alone so that nothing and no-one can confuse and distract you. He realizes that because of your emotional connection, as long as they are still living, you will not be as fully committed to the plans He has for you!

Avoid the Seductive Noise in the World

It is a wonderful thing to know Christ as your Savior and your protector. But many of us stop there. We read the Word about loving our neighbors and trying to be an example and unfortunately, we quickly get satisfied with our Christian journey. We have not been taught the importance in growing in your relationship with Christ. It is easy to see and stay motivated in our walk with Christ. The closer you get to the Father, the deeper your obligations become. We realize that much of our walk with Him expands our comfort zone and what we would naturally want to do. *But the truth is the closer we get to Him, the more He expects from us.* The bottom line is, we must see things differently. If we want to change the world, everything must change!

We are not taught to see things differently. In most churches our faith is described to us in a language and a mindset we can understand. We rarely start looking at our role and what we are commissioned to do to change the world! Yes, it is one of the hardest things to not get caught up and dependent on our life here on Earth. Besides, the Earth is very enticing. As much violence and uncertainty, it brings, the Earth also brings power, money and glamour. There is constantly a seducing noise all the time an everywhere, here on Earth. The enemy is busy trying to make the noise around you more and more tempting and louder than ever. The goal is to distract you from God and your walk with Him. It is common for us to be tempted and to desire things from the world, but Christ is very clear that we should desire Him the most. Nothing in our life should compare to the relationship that we should have with Him.

Yes, we are humans, and this life is what we have come to know. But as hard as we work to keep things flowing smoothly, we need to sanctify our every day by learning how to think about two things at once. We can't ignore the noise of the world completely because we still must function in it. Therefore, to sanctify our everyday we need to split our mind and our focus. We should put part of our mind on our everyday obligations and how we are presenting ourselves to society. While remaining guarded knowing that we are in a spiritual war and have an invisible fight attached to us as we go throughout our day. The objective of the fight is to take away our relationship with Christ. The enemy is desperately trying to prove Him wrong in everything that He has promised. Now many people would argue that we are not able to fully focus on two things at once.

Having a two-way focus is a process and it takes having a strong relationship with the Father but it is indeed possible. *Allow everything you do on earth to be for the Glory of Christ, every relationship you have, every word you speak and every action you take.*

Suffering - Sanctify your future and guard any future suffering that makes you understand that our mission on Earth is temporary and all of us are just here for a moment. Although we get attached to people and things, everything we attach ourselves to is temporary. As your life continues, in every role you play, see yourself as purpose–filled first. For example: You may be a mother with a Godly purpose, a schoolteacher with a purpose, or an accountant with a purpose. But the secret is to see

*your purpose first and then acknowledge that you are
also a mother, schoolteacher, or an accountant. Let
your role on Earth be secondary, not first. Let God be
the biggest and most important part of you in everything
you do so that you can sanctify your future suffering,
with more God than pain.*

Change our perspective: What is huge to us is small to God!

We can't undo the human out of us!! For example, it is
hard to not panic when we are shocked with a problem.

*If only we could see things the way that Christ sees
them, we would not worry or fret about anything.*

Let's say that life is going and moving at regular speed
and then suddenly, we are devastated by a person or a
circumstance. The bigger the problem, the more out of
control things seem. We need to sanctify our everyday
by asking the Father to help us see things as He sees
them. This might be hard to understand so let me further
explain. Not having enough money to pay your rent is

huge to us but small to God. Getting fired from your job can be devastating to us but small to God.

See, when problems arise, we tend to look at the here and the now. If you were to get fired, there are a lot of emotions you are experiencing. You would probably be embarrassed, hurt, shocked, and concerned about finding a new job. But when Christ examines the situation, nothing shocks Him because He knew that you were going to be fired before you even started that job. In fact, He may have initiated you leaving that job so that he can bless you in a position that includes your purpose! No one knows the why and the hows, but one thing we do know is that God deals with our now and present-day based on what He has planned for your future.

*Let me repeat this, what is huge to us, is very small to God because He directs our life not based on where you are now, but instead were you are going in the future.

It is never about today, and it is always about tomorrow. If we could just learn this perspective in our

Christian journey, nothing and no-one will ever be able to influence our faith again!!

Suffering - God is a master planner. He will often allow situations to happen so that you can grasp something more important in your future. Let's consider this, He may allow you to lose your young child in a car accident. When you think of this, all you can comprehend is that your beautiful child is dead and that he/she did not deserve death! You wonder if you are being punished by God. Although this is devastating and the pain is indescribable, God may have allowed the death to happen because He knew you would never become who you are purposed to be if your child was alive. *Sometimes God must move people out of the way!* Although you have been a very serious Christian for years. Due to the habit of "child worship" you would have allowed your child to pull you away from your faith and prayer life. You would have never guessed that your love for your child needed balance and realism. You just thought you were loving your child and trying to make him/her happy. But unfortunately, your child was your earthly God who you put more energy into than your relationship with Christ. Although as humans we make this mistake constantly, the purpose God has for you will only work if you only serve

Him and learn to put some distance and between you, your child and everyone else.

We look at our pain and hurt from a "right now" perspective. God positions our life based on who and what we need to become in the future.

And looking into your future God knew that because your child was worshipped instead of taught, he/she would grow up to be a menace to society. Their presence would have caused problem after problem. So, God spared you the pain. God took your child early to heaven because otherwise, he/she would have destroyed your life and theirs!

See Everything and Everyone as a Potential Distraction!

I realize that this title may seem somewhat harsh and impossible to do. Some might even think that I made a mistake in my wording and that there is no way I could mean "everything and everyone." This may seem ridiculous and beyond how we as humans believe we can possibly live. But the bottom line is nothing in that title is a mistake or over exaggerated!

Listen closely, as humans we have a problem with balance. Many times, we either love something way too much that it becomes our everything or dislike something to the point of making it a sin because we keep obsessing over it.

Listen closely, most of us realize that when we are attracted or have a strong interest in something, we often think about it so much that it goes into our mindset, and it gets twisted and unbalanced in our thought life. At this level, we tend to overthink and make more of it than what it is worth. Even when we are ready to move on and think about other things we often don't know how to control our thoughts so we allow it to stay alive in our mind. The more attracted we are to it the more complex the twist becomes and the harder it is to think about other things. Now don't get me wrong, while living here, we will always like and love things. God has given us the ability to have a personality that reflects what we are attracted to. Although He did not have to, God designed the world to give us pleasure and enjoyment, while we are here on assignment. One of the things that separate us and make us uniquely different from each other is our personal preference.

He did not give us the ability to like and love things to go to the extreme and feel as if we can't live without it. When we allow this to happen, then we are close to idolatry. Our ability to be attracted to other things is not supposed to replace Him! It is supposed to make us more in awe of God for allowing us the beautiful emotion to feel.

The interesting thing is that when our mind is twisted with ugly, negative and revengeful thoughts the power of the twist becomes much more robust and complex. Many of us don't realize it but too many of us have compromised to live in a constant negative state. We don't fight the fight to stay positive and encouraged. Many of us choose to allow our emotions to control everything! Sometimes our attitude is worse than other times, but more than we realize it, we have the tendency to allow our mind to stay in a place of bitterness. Many of us do this without being aware of it. We become so distracted with the challenges of the world, the place of unthankfulness becomes part of who we are.

Please understand, the act of being unthankful is simply missing the opportunity to be thankful. Feeling nothing about your blessings is being unthankful.

Unfortunately, the world feeds and encourages this mindset because the world gravitated and grows on negativity. This is how we become closer and closer to the personality of our society and farther away from the personality of Christ.

The more distracted we are the more worldly we become! Let's remember that the enemy specialize in evil. Therefore, he is highly delighted when we allow negativity to live in us. He has a way of quickly moving this destructive energy through us so it can turn into multiple negative emotions. When we allow bad thoughts and beliefs to reign in us it heavily effect our confidence, self-worth and level of faith. It is impossible to keep your mind constantly on God when your connection to Him is unconnected.

Negativity is surprisingly seductive. Our feelings can become so complex, we often forget what first caused the distraction initially. We just know that all of a sudden, we feel mad, depressed and hopeless.

The enemy wants our love to turn into a self-destructive obsession that can never be reached. And our dislike to transform into an ugly hate that separates us from the love of God.

It is interesting how we can hear multiple compliments from many people but if we get one negative comment, we become fixated and we overanalyze the one unfavorable response. We play the comment over and over in our head. Oftentimes, only through passing time allows the flushing out the hurt. Negative energy is more powerful than what we realize, and it quickly spreads into other toxic things.

Negativity is a distraction that compounds into other things. It will snatch you up and tempt you to think bad, be bad and to conclude bad things.

You can't think about the goodness of God and think ugly and jealous thoughts at the same time!

The emotion of negativity flows quickly and constantly through us because the world inhabits and feeds on negativity. It is ironic but the way it multiplies in us is also how it advances in the world.

Some may believe that it seems unchristian to label their child, spouse, and parents as a distraction. Let us not forget that God is love, and the emotion of love comes directly from Him. Of course, God wants us to love our children and family members. He also allows us to have an uncompromising passion towards them. But as hard as it may be, He does not want us to idolize our children, spouse, parents, or friends. It is very easy to put the wants and the needs of others higher than Gods. If we challenge and monitor what we say and what we do, we would be shocked how often we give more energy and awareness to those closes to us, than we do to our awesome Savior. Yes, we try and try but most of us slip daily in our choices. If we just look at the widespread behavior of people-pleasing. Too many of us would lie or do something we really don't want to do, to not disappoint others. The destructive behavior of pleasing others has become such a massive problem that it is seen in every culture and every age group. It is like a worldwide plague which often breeds low self-esteem and doubt. When we lie and say we want to do something we really don't want to do, we are choosing to disappoint God by lying than disappointing our loved one.

Suffering - When it comes to the ones we love deeply, we suffer. We can hurt so hard for them that it is difficult to go on. Especially when it comes to our children, many of us don't see any purpose to keep living if they are not living too. It is easy to be overprotective and over involved in our children's life to the point that we don't leave any space for Christ to enter our relationship with them. Although suffering is a natural response, the Father does not want us to lose all hope for living when someone we love dies. *We are not living for them; we are living to fulfill our purpose for Christ.* He makes it clear that we should love Him the most. He does not want to be number 2 in any of our lives. He wants us to love our children completely but not worship them. Instead of being obsessed with the people that are closes to us, He wants us to trust Him and pray for the life of the ones we love the most.

When we sanctify our preparation by not allowing anything to become more important than God, we will be blessed. When we allow Him to be our number 1 all the time, through the good and the bad times we are not trying to quickly make Him the most important when hard times come.

When it comes to our loved ones, we have very limited resources of what we can do for them. We can feel sorry for them, cry with them, but in most cases, we can't fix or help their situation. What I am saying is, we only have prayer to give to them anyway. Our only answer is God. So instead of allowing others to get the best of you. Let's purposefully live where we are giving God the total best of us, despite what we are going through. So, when life gets unbearable, we don't have to piece back together our relationship with God that we allowed distractions to almost destroy.

TO MY READERS…

To my readers, it is my prayer that this book meets you exactly where you are at. That it will speak to you and through you. It is my hope that it will be a comfort and a resource that you can go back to repeatedly when things seem unbearable.

I realize that much of this content may not be what you normally would expect. But it is my objective to give new ways to think, act and be, when it comes to our relationship with our Father. I hope that you feel challenged to sanctify everything. Do more and be better regardless of your present level in Christ.

God is calling us to be more and give more. We are either serious about our walk or we aren't. The faith we had twenty years ago will not be enough in this sick and increasingly violent world. All around us people are changing, and they are becoming more and more bold in how they feel, and how they act. There is a rude dominance that is taking over our society. You can spot it when you see them driving 100 mph in a 20-mph school zone with absolutely no thought of any of the people or children around them. And if they are stopped by the police, they are the first one to pull out a gun. And demand a confrontation. Trying to defend their unmindful wrongness. As Christians, we can't afford to be left behind. We must become bolder and more fearless also to reach this new dominant behavior. We must be bold in who we are and what we believe.

It is time that we move beyond re-explaining the basics. We need to strive to focus on growing and getting higher in Christ. It is time that we stop being satisfied with the same level of faith and reciting the same prayers repeatedly. Listen, if we are making sure that nothing and no-one comes before Christ, so we are already reading the word and consistently praying. In our journey it is hard to do one thing without the other. We need to work on being more usable to God. And we should be working on fixing areas that are a challenge for us. As I mentioned earlier, we have the tendency to get too comfortable with Him. We have learned to be satisfied with a mediocre life in Christ. We go to church every Sunday; we are kind to others, and we pray before every meal. In doing this we feel that we are living the life of a good Christian. We rarely think about how to get to the next level in Christ, many of us are too comfortable where we are at. We are spoiled because God rescues us regardless of what we do. Many of us casually floa   t on His grace through the good and the bad.

How you live your life determines how deep you will suffer.

As I close, I want to acknowledge again that suffering is horrific. It is a time that we can clearly know how strong we are at our lowest point. During this time, God wants us to lay back and allow Him to comfort and speak to us. Not allowing negative talk to enter in. Even if we can only say a few words like: "help me Father, help me Father", over and over again, He wants us to totally look to Him for our reason to keep living. Even in the midst of severe grieving, He wants us to have His promises on our mind more than the pain that we feel.

He does not want us to diminish Him as we suffer. He wants to be bigger and more anchored than ever before!

Lynette Costner,

Author